THE LIFE OF XXXTENTACION

THE LIFE OF XXXTENTACION

BLAZE CARTER

CONTENTS

TO ZFD

For opening my eyes to the genius of XXXTentacion. Your passion for his music helped me appreciate the layers emotion in his work. Through our conversations, I learned not just about the artist, but about the struggles and triumphs of a generation that resonates with his message. Your dedication to his artistry inspired me to dive deeper int his life and legacy. Thank you for inspiring me to understand the chaotic brilliant XXXTentacion and the connection he forged with so many.

Acknowledgement

I want to give a huge shout-out to the design collective Real Fashion Bomb and the gallery *Florida Man* for permitting me to reuse my artworks in this book. Your support means the world to me and has added so much to the stories I wanted to tell. Thanks for being a part of this journey and for championing the creative spirit that XXXTentacion embodied.

CHAPTER 1

A Controversial Icon

The story of XXXTentacion begins in chaos, and it's a chaos he never quite escaped. Born Jahseh Dwayne Ricardo Onfroy in 1998, XXXTentacion rocketed to fame in the latter half of the 2010s as a rapper whose music was as turbulent and troubled as the man himself.

His songs, marked by a raw emotional vulnerability that spoke directly to a generation riddled with anxiety and rage, tapped into the darker corners of youth culture. Yet for every tear shed by his fans, there was a fist raised in anger and a desire for redemption.

His rapid rise to stardom came with accusations of domestic violence, brutal beatings, and a string of legal battles that left many wondering if he was the artist of a generation or a figure that embodied its darkest impulses.

In the years since his murder in 2018, XXXTentacion's name has become a byword for contradiction. He remains a figure who splits opinion, with critics focusing on his violent past while his most ardent fans maintain he was a reflection of his generation and on a path to redemption.

His popularity has only grown since his death, as posthumous releases, fan tributes, and continued cultural resonance have kept his name alive. But can we, or should we, separate the art from the artist? What can we learn about ourselves by looking at his life and legacy?

So that is the central question: can we extract the deeply personal, often heart-wrenching music from the man who, in the public eye, embodied some of the worst impulses of youth violence and recklessness? For many, XXXTentacion represents a paradox, an artist whose ability to connect with fans on issues like depression, loneliness, and suicide was matched only by his capacity for cruelty and destruction. His legacy, as much a product of his brief but explosive life as his tragic death, forces us to confront these 21st century American contradictions head-on.

In the landscape of modern rap, few figures loom as large and as controversial as XXXTentacion. The public's fascination with him is a testament to his ability to provoke people—and provoke he did, both in his music and in his actions. From the earliest days of his career, he stood apart from his peers. His breakthrough single, "Look at Me!," was a chaotic anthem of sex, power, macho violence, distortion, a raw expression of teenage angst that became an instant hit. With lyrics like: I'm like "Bitch, who is your man's?", ayy / Can't keep my dick in my pants, ayy," it was brash, aggressive, obnoxious, and unapologetically confrontational, qualities that defined not only the song but XXXTentacion himself. Here was a rapper who didn't just reflect the emotions and desires of a generation; he embodied them. At the same time, we have to recognize where this style of thinking, acting, talking and singing came from. In a country that continually glorifies and rewards these orientations, who can be shocked by this hit?

So it was the same qualities that made his music resonate with fans, however, that fueled the controversies that surrounded him. While XXXTentacion was gaining fans for his emotional openness, particularly around mental health, his personal life told a darker story. Accusations of domestic violence and assault followed him, culminating in a 2016 arrest for the brutal beating of his then-girlfriend, Geneva Ayala.

The details of the case were harrowing, painting a portrait of a man capable of terrible acts. For many, it was impossible to reconcile this image of violence with the artist who sang openly about his own vulnerabilities, who in songs like "Jocelyn Flores" and "Sad!" seemed to offer a window into the pain and suffering of a generation.

As XXXTentacion's star continued to rise, the conversation around him became increasingly polarized. His most devoted fans—many of them young, marginalized, and perhaps struggling with their own mental health—saw him as a hero, someone who spoke to their pain in a way no one else did. The context of this was in many ways the opening up of social media and other digital technologies that were simultaneously opening the world to young people while also making them feel ever more isolated and like they were never enough (a theme that would be openly addressed in Greta Gerwig's 2023 Barbie movie, where Ryan Gosling plays Ken, whose "Kenough" hoodie became its own Tik-Tok fashion statement).

His detractors (and there were many), on the other hand, saw him as a danger, a figure who glorified violence and set a toxic example for his audience. And perhaps most troublingly, his success appeared to show that violent behavior could be excused—or even rewarded—in the music industry. His career, marked by chart-topping success and equally headline-grabbing scandal, became a symbol of the contradictions inherent in celebrity culture, where fame and notoriety often go hand in hand. Why this conduct by XXXtentacion garnered so much negative attention when similar, and much worse, acts by so many others were glossed over remains a mystery.

At the heart of the debate over XXXTentacion's legacy is the question of whether we can separate his art from his crimes. This is not a new question—our culture has long grappled with the separation of the artist from their actions, particularly when those actions involve violence.

Maybe it is because in the case of XXXTentacion, the stakes feel higher. His music was not just a product of his environment; it was a reflection of his inner turmoil, a soundtrack to the self-destructive path he seemed destined to walk. His songs were confessional, often deeply personal, offering a glimpse into his mental state in a way that felt both raw and real.

A related question is whether the art can stand on its own when the artist is so deeply entangled in violence? Can we appreciate songs like "17," where he explores themes of depression and hopelessness, knowing that the man behind the music was accused of some of the very behaviors he seemed to decry? For some, the answer is a resounding yes. They argue that his music should be judged on its own merits, that the emotional connection he forged with millions of fans cannot be dismissed because of his personal failings. For others, his crimes overshadow any artistic achievements, and to celebrate his music is to condone the violence he perpetrated.

In many ways, the debate over XXXTentacion mirrors broader societal discussions about accountability, forgiveness, and the role of art in shaping our culture. His life and legacy force us to confront uncomfortable questions about the relationship between an artist and their work, and whether we can—or should—draw a line between the two. Jean Genet, Flannery O Conner, Ezra Pound, Caravaggio and so many other great figures from the pantheon of great artists and writers have left a complicated legacy, as their art often stands in stark contrast to the turbulent, sometimes destructive ideas they promoted or lives they led.

Perhaps the most compelling aspect of XXXTentacion's story is the way it encapsulates the contradictions of fame in the digital age. He was, at once, a villain and a victim, a product of his circumstances and a force of his own making. His music spoke to the insecurities and fears of a generation, yet his actions often betrayed the very values he claimed to represent.

In songs like "Changes" and "Everybody Dies in Their Nightmares," XXXTentacion laid bare his own struggles with depression, loneliness, and the fear of abandonment. His fans saw in him a kindred spirit, someone who understood the pain they were going through because he had lived it too. But alongside this vulnerability was a darker, more destructive side. His violent outbursts, both in his personal life and in his interactions with the media, painted a picture of a man at war with himself and the world around him. Fame, for XXXTentacion, was both a blessing and a curse—it gave him a platform to express his deepest emotions, but it also amplified the strange times that had defined his life from the start.

In the end, the story of XXXTentacion is one of contradictions—between fame and violence, vulnerability and destruction, art and crime. His music continues to resonate with millions of fans, even as his legacy remains mired in controversy. As we look back on his life, we are left with the difficult task of making sense of these contradictions, of finding a way to understand the artist without excusing the man. In this way, XXXTentacion remains one of the most compelling and divisive figures of his generation—a man whose life and music defy easy categorization, and whose legacy forces us to confront the uncomfortable realities of fame, violence, and mental health in the modern age.

CHAPTER 2

Jahseh Onfroy

From the start, XXXTentacion was a study in contradictions. Born Jahseh Dwayne Ricardo Onfroy on January 23, 1998, in Plantation, Florida, his life began in the shadows of violence and instability. South Florida, with its strange mix of sun-drenched beauty and dark undercurrents of crime, would be the backdrop of his early years. It was a landscape of extremes, and he would come to define that in his music. Jahseh Onfroy grew up as part of a generation raised by single mothers, absent fathers, and systemic inequality, where life was often a battle for survival. His own story reads like the beginning of an American tragedy, one in which all roads seem to lead toward some kind of self-destruction.

As a child, Onfroy was restless, full of pent-up energy and aggression that could not be contained. Reports from those who knew him describe a young boy who was always in trouble—fights at school, conflicts at home. His mother, Cleo, was a single parent who worked multiple jobs to support him, and she struggled to control his temper. "He was always a difficult child," she said in a rare interview after his death, a note of weariness in her voice. "He was fighting from the day he was born." The roots of his anger, she explained, could be traced back to the absence of his father, who was in and out of jail for most of Jahseh's life. Without a stable male figure, Jahseh grew up in the rougher neighborhoods of Broward County, where violence, bravado, and chaos were the currency of survival.

By the time he reached his teenage years, the world around him had taught Jahseh some hard lessons about power and control. He learned that, in order to survive, you had to strike first and strike hard. Violence became his shield and his weapon, a way to project strength in a world that had denied him any semblance of real control. This fight-or-flight sense of survival bled into his music, where themes of violence, anger, and betrayal would become central. He never fit in, and he didn't want to. Instead, he embraced the role of the outcast, cultivating a persona that resonated with legions of disillusioned youth who saw their own struggles reflected in his songs.

Onfroy's adolescence was littered with moments of profound disruption. Expelled from middle school for fighting, he bounced between friends' houses and juvenile detention centers. By 16, he had developed a reputation for violence—both feared and admired by his peers. His behavior was a product of both nature and nurture; one of the most defining moment of his early life was his time in juvenile detention. It was here that Onfroy's identity began to crystallize. Surrounded by other young men who shared his anger and brokenness, he hardened.

Stories from this period paint a picture of a boy who had learned to use violence as a language. In interviews later in his life, he would speak of it as a necessity, a way to keep himself safe from those who would try to hurt him first. These institutional factors have shaped an entire generation of kids who, for a variety of reasons, find themselves behind walls and bars.

In the detention center, Onfroy also met Stokeley Clevon Goulbourne, who would later become Ski Mask the Slump God. The two bonded over their mutual love for music, and in this unlikely environment, Onfroy began to consider music as a potential escape from the life he seemed destined to lead. It was during this period that Jahseh Onfroy became XXXTentacion—a name that would soon take on a life of its own. "I was always violent," he admitted in one of his rare interviews, "but music became my way of channeling that aggression."

From the beginning, XXXTentacion's music reflected the lack of order of his life. His early tracks, released on Sound-Cloud, were raw and unpolished, full of distorted beats and shouted lyrics. Listening to these tracks gave you the feeling that you heard him, especially when compared to the legions of over-edited, auto-tuned, overproduced works that are commercially available. And it was this rawness that attracted a devoted fanbase. His early music wasn't just about anger—it was anger, distilled into sound. For many of his fans, who came from similarly troubled backgrounds, XXXTentacion was a reflection of their own pain, their own frustration, their own sense of alienation. In him, they saw someone who understood what it was like to be pushed to the margins, to be dismissed by society. As his following grew, so too did the myth of XXXTentacion—the anti-hero who had clawed his way up from the depths, bloodied but unbowed.

In crafting the persona of XXXTentacion, Onfroy tapped into a rich cultural history of the outsider, the rebel, the harlequin. Like the punk rockers of the 1970s or the grunge musicians of the 1990s, he positioned himself as a voice for the voiceless, an artist who didn't play by the rules because the rules were never made for people like him. And really, they weren't.

From the earliest days of his career, he presented himself as someone who stood outside of the system, unafraid to challenge authority. His appearance—a strange blend of goth, punk, and rap aesthetics—reflected this rebellion. With his shock of bleached blonde hair, facial tattoos, and somber expression, XXXTentacion looked every bit the tortured artist, the young man at war with the world. Of course, it did not hurt that he is also beautiful by almost any standards.

This persona wasn't just an act—it was an extension of Jahseh Onfroy's own life. He didn't just play the role of the outsider; he was the outsider. His early experiences with the criminal justice system, his tumultuous relationships, and his struggles with identity all fed into the image he projected. He was open about his battles with depression and suicidal thoughts, using his music as a platform to talk about the struggles that so many of his fans shared. Songs like "Jocelyn Flores" and "Everybody Dies in Their Nightmares" tackled these themes head-on, and it was this emotional vulnerability that made XXXTentacion a beacon for young people dealing with their own mental health issues.

For his fans, XXXTentacion was more than just a rapper—he was a symbol of survival, someone who had been through the fire and come out the other side. His openness about his worries resonated with a generation that was increasingly vocal about these issues, and his music became a space where they could confront their own pain. "He was the first artist I ever heard who made me feel like it was okay to be depressed," one fan wrote on Reddit after his death. "His music saved my life."

Enter "Look at Me!" XXXTentacion's breakout hit. This song that propelled him from the underground SoundCloud scene into the mainstream consciousness. Released in 2015, the track is a sonic assault—a blast of distorted bass and shouted lyrics that feels less like a song and more like a primal scream. The track's aggression is palpable, its energy frenetic and unrelenting. In many ways, "Look at Me!" encapsulates everything that XXXTentacion was as an artist—angry, rebellious, and unapologetically raw.

Lyrically, "Look at Me!" is confrontational, a declaration of independence from the norms of both society and the music industry. "Can't keep my dick in my pants," he shouts in the opening lines, setting the tone for a track that is as vulgar as it is defiant. This is not a song that plays by the rules, and that is precisely the point. XXXTentacion isn't interested in fitting in—he wants to break the mold, to tear down the expectations that have been placed on him as a young Black man in America. The song's explicit content, while shocking to some, is a deliberate act of rebellion. It's XXXTentacion's way of saying, "I don't care what you think of me."

The song's production is equally aggressive, with its distorted bass and chaotic beats creating a sense of disorientation. There's a direct texture to the sound that feels almost unpolished, as though it was recorded in a fit of rage. This lack of refinement is part of what made the song so appealing to fans. It didn't feel like a sanitized product made for the radio—it felt real, a burst of unfiltered emotion that tapped into the anger and frustration so many young people were feeling.

"Look at Me!" became an anthem for disaffected youth, a rallying cry for those who felt ignored by society. In the song's aggression, they found a reflection of their own anger, their own sense of being pushed to the margins. "He was speaking for all of us," one fan wrote on Twitter after the song went viral. "He was saying the things we were too afraid to say."

The success of "Look at Me!" was not just about the music—it was about what the song represented. For fans, it was a rejection of the mainstream, a middle finger to the system that had left them feeling abandoned. In XXXTentacion, they found an artist who wasn't afraid to be different, who wasn't afraid to express the anger and pain they themselves felt. The song's aggression was a catharsis for listeners who felt they had no other outlet for their emotions.

But what does this tell us about XXXTentacion's audience? In some ways, "Look at Me!" is a reflection of the disillusionment felt by a generation growing up in a world that seems increasingly hostile. This is a generation raised on social media, where image is everything, and yet they feel invisible. They are told to aspire to success, yet they are often left with few avenues to achieve it. In "Look at Me!," XXXTentacion gives voice to this frustration, this feeling of being ignored, frustrated, and overlooked. The song's aggression is not just a form of dissent—it is a cry for attention, a demand to be seen in a world that so often looks the other way.

For a lot of XXXTentacion's fans, this sense of rebellion, this refusal to conform, is what made him an anti-hero. He wasn't perfect, and he didn't pretend to be. He was messy, flawed, and at times destructive. But in his imperfection, his fans saw something real, something and someone they could relate to. In a world that often demanded perfection, XXXTentacion's willingness to be unapologetically himself, to embrace his own darkness, was a source of comfort for those who felt like they didn't belong.

As we look back at the making of XXXTentacion, it becomes clear that his rise was about more than just music. He represented something deeper—a rebellion against the expectations placed on young people in a world that often feels indifferent to their struggles. He was the anti-hero they didn't know they needed, and in his music, they found a voice for their own pain.

CHAPTER 3

The Rise of a New Sound

There was something different about XXXTentacion. You could hear it from the first seconds of a track like "Jocelyn Flores," where the haunting, fragile guitar loop drags you into the song's aching melancholy before you've even considered the lyrics. It was this sound, both understated and direct, that set him apart from so many of his peers. XXXTentacion blurred lines—between genres, between his own pain and public persona, and perhaps most notably, between what was real and what was performative. He made it difficult to know where the artist ended and the person began, and it was in that ambiguity where his influence, and his controversy, lived.

It's hard to categorize XXXTentacion's music without reducing it to something that doesn't quite capture what made it unique. For an artist who rose to prominence during the reign of SoundCloud rap—a genre known for its lo-fi production, distorted bass, and raw, unpolished delivery—XXXTentacion stood out precisely because he refused to adhere to any one sound.

In one moment, his voice was a snarl of anger, as in his breakout track "Look at Me!"; in another, it was a quiet whisper, as if he were speaking directly into your ear, as in "Jocelyn Flores." His music pulled from everywhere—emo, punk, rap, even grunge. He created a collage of sound that shouldn't have worked but somehow did.

To understand his rise is to understand the cultural moment that birthed it. In the late 2010s, hip-hop was evolving. Artists like Drake, Travis Scott, and Kendrick Lamar were pushing the genre's boundaries, but something different was happening on the internet, specifically on SoundCloud, where a new wave of underground artists was emerging.

These artists weren't getting radio play or major label deals, but they didn't need to. The platform allowed them to cultivate fanbases through direct connection with listeners, bypassing traditional music industry gatekeepers. It was DIY in the most visceral sense. And of all the artists on SoundCloud, XXXTentacion was one of the most compelling.

What set XXXTentacion apart wasn't just his sound, though. It was the power of his emotion. In a scene dominated by hard beats and braggadocio, XXXTentacion's music was introspective, often painfully so.

Take "Jocelyn Flores," for example. This track is less a rap song than a eulogy. Named after a friend of XXXTentacion's who had committed suicide, the song explores the intersection of grief, guilt, and depression. Over a somber, looping guitar riff, XXXTentacion's voice is low, almost monotone, as if he's drained of the energy to feel anything but numb. "I'm in pain, wanna put ten shots in my brain," he confesses, his voice devoid of the performative swagger that often accompanies lyrics like these in mainstream rap. There's no posturing here, no attempt to be cool or detached. It's pure sadness, laid bare for anyone who cares to listen.

But to what extent was this vulnerability genuine? And to what extent was it calculated, a performance meant to endear him to his young, impressionable audience? This question lingered over XXXTentacion's career and continues to follow his legacy. In many ways, he was the perfect artist for the era of social media, where authenticity is both craved and elusive. He bared his soul online, in interviews, on Instagram Live, and in his music, but there was always the sense that he was curating this image of himself, that he knew how to manipulate the emotions of his audience. "He was like an open wound," one fan said in a Reddit thread after his death. "But I think he wanted us to see the wound, to feel bad for him."

For fans, though, whether or not XXXTentacion's vulnerability was performative seemed beside the point. His music spoke to them in a way that few artists' music did. In a time when mental health struggles were increasingly being destigmatized, XXXTentacion's openness about his own battles with depression, suicidal thoughts, and trauma resonated deeply. For many young listeners, his music was not just relatable but cathartic, a way to process their own pain. "Jocelyn Flores" became an anthem for anyone who had ever felt the weight of loss or the burden of their own mental health. And for some, it was more than just a song. It was a lifeline.

Yet, for all the sincerity in songs like "Jocelyn Flores," it's impossible to ignore the more cynical aspects of XXXTentacion's career. He was, after all, a super savvy marketer, someone who understood how to manipulate the media and his audience. He knew that controversy sold, and he used that to his advantage. His violent past—including allegations of domestic abuse and a viral video of him hitting a woman—was well-documented, and yet it only seemed to fuel his fame. There's a sense that, for XXXTentacion, these moments of personal failings were part of the performance, part of what made him compelling to his fans. It's as if the line between the artist and the persona, between real life and the spectacle of his public image, was blurred beyond recognition.

Take his role in the rise of SoundCloud rap, for instance. The genre itself was rebellious, rejecting the polished, commercial sound of mainstream hip-hop in favor of something messier, angrier, more immediate. It was music for the disaffected, for those who felt overlooked by the traditional music industry. XXXTentacion thrived in this environment because he was able to embody that sense of rebellion. But unlike many of his peers, whose lyrics centered around drugs, partying, and violence, XXXTentacion's music often touched on themes of self doubt and vulnerability. He offered something more than just anger—he offered a kind of emotional release.

But how much of this vulnerability was real? Even in his more introspective tracks, there's a sense that XXXTentacion was performing for an audience. His lyrics, while raw, often feel calculated, as if he's saying exactly what he knows will resonate with his listeners. In "Jocelyn Flores," he sings about guilt and depression in a way that is both deeply personal and universally relatable. "I know you're somewhere, somewhere / I've been trapped in my mind, girl, just holdin' on," he croons in the chorus. It's a sentiment that could apply to anyone who has ever felt the weight of grief or mental illness. But it's also a sentiment that feels carefully crafted, designed to strike a chord with the millions of young people who have experienced those same feelings.

And perhaps that's the point. Whether or not XXXTentacion's vulnerability was performative, it doesn't change the fact that it resonated with his audience. In a world where so many artists seem disconnected from their fans, XXXTentacion offered something different.

So, he wasn't just a rapper; he was a conduit for his listeners' emotions. He didn't just make music about pain—he made music that felt like pain, that took the listener into the depths of his own psyche. In doing so, he created a space for his fans to confront their own demons.

It's worth considering the larger cultural forces at play here, too. XXXTentacion rose to prominence at a time when discussions about mental health were becoming more mainstream, particularly among younger generations. His music tapped into a growing movement of artists—like Kid Cudi, Logic, and Lil Peep—who were using their platforms to talk openly about depression, anxiety, and suicide.

In this context, XXXTentacion's vulnerability didn't just feel authentic—it felt necessary. He was giving voice to a generation that was struggling with its own new cultural landscape, a generation that was increasingly disillusioned with traditional ideas of masculinity and emotional stoicism.

But there's also something troubling about the way XXXTentacion presented his pain. In songs like "Jocelyn Flores," he seems to wallow in his depression, offering little in the way of resolution or hope. It's a stark contrast to someone like Kid Cudi, whose music often feels like a journey toward healing. For XXXTentacion, there is no healing—only pain. This, too, resonated with his fans, many of whom were drawn to the darkness in his music. But it also raises questions about the impact of his art. Was he helping his listeners confront their own pain, or was he glorifying it? Was he offering catharsis, or was he feeding into a cycle of despair?

The answer, perhaps, lies somewhere in between. For some fans, XXXTentacion's music was undoubtedly therapeutic. It gave them a space to feel seen, to feel understood. For others, it may have reinforced their own feelings of hopelessness. But to focus solely on the impact of his music is to ignore the larger questions about who XXXTentacion was as an artist, and what he represented.

At the heart of his music, and his life really, was a deep sense of contradiction. He was truly vulnerable and violent, both sincere and performative. His music was unsanitized and underproduced, but it was also carefully constructed. He blurred the lines between genres, between authenticity and artifice, between himself and his audience. In doing so, he created a new kind of sound—one that was as complex and contradictory as the man behind it.

And perhaps that's why XXXTentacion continues to be such a divisive figure. For some, he was a revolutionary artist, someone who pushed the boundaries of what rap could be. For others, he was a deeply flawed individual, whose personal demons often overshadowed his artistic achievements.

But regardless of where one falls on that spectrum, there's no denying his impact. In blending emo, rap, punk, and his own personal pain, XXXTentacion created a sound that was uniquely his own—a sound that continues to influence the landscape of music today.

CHAPTER 4

SoundCloud and Beyond

In the era of SoundCloud and Instagram, fame is something that can be built—or destroyed—at light speed. For XXXTentacion, the internet was both his rocket fuel and his downfall, the stage upon which his meteoric rise and violent, public unraveling took place.

He seemed to have understood, almost intuitively, how to manipulate social media to craft a narrative, one that blurred the lines between real life and spectacle, between violence and vulnerability. And for better or worse, this understanding was central to his success.

To speak of XXXTentacion's career without considering the role of social media is impossible. His rise was almost entirely predicated on it. Platforms like SoundCloud and YouTube allowed him to bypass traditional music industry gatekeepers, reaching listeners directly in their bedrooms, on their phones, late at night when they were most vulnerable to his haunting, raw sound. But it was Instagram and Twitter where he built his persona—the troubled, tormented anti-hero who oscillated between extremes of emotion, between outbursts of violence and moments of heartbreaking tenderness.

In many ways, XXXTentacion was a product of his time. The late 2010s were a period where the boundaries between public and private, artist and individual, were dissolving in real time. Social media platforms had turned celebrities into constant, living content, their every move available for public consumption.

For someone like XXXTentacion, whose life was as chaotic and complicated as his music, this was both an opportunity and a danger. I suspect this is true for all of Gen Z today.

There's an often-repeated notion that if it bleeds, it ledes....controversy sells. In XXXTentacion's case, it wasn't just that controversy sold—it became the main currency by which he traded his fame. His online presence was marked by a kind of instability that felt genuine, even if it was often unclear how much of it was theatrical.

He was often unpredictable. One day, he would post a video apologizing to his fans for his violent past; the next, he would be caught on camera in a brutal brawl. The volatility of his persona was captivating, even if it was disturbing. It was a kind of car crash fame—people watched because they couldn't look away.

At the same time, social media offered him a way to communicate directly with his audience in a way that felt personal, even intimate. His Instagram Lives were often long, rambling affairs, where he would talk about his struggles with emotional turmoil, his regrets, his fears. These moments of confession made him seem real in a way that many artists do not. "He spoke to us like he knew what we were going through," one fan recalled on Twitter after his death. "It wasn't polished or scripted. It felt like he was just as lost as we were."

But there was always a darker side to this accessibility. While social media allowed XXXTentacion to connect with fans, it also exposed him to constant scrutiny, amplifying the controversies that followed him. His frequent outbursts, his unhinged behavior, and his legal troubles became fodder for tabloids and gossip blogs, creating a feedback loop where the more outrageous his actions, the more attention he received. It didn't matter if the attention was negative; in the world of social media, any attention was good attention.

There's a moment from his career that captures this dynamic perfectly. In 2016, XXXTentacion was arrested for the assault of his then-pregnant girlfriend, Geneva Ayala, an act of violence so horrific that it seemed like it would end his career before it had even really begun. But instead of fading into obscurity, XXXTentacion doubled down on his persona as the tortured, misunderstood artist.

So, he didn't shy away from the allegations—instead, he leaned into them, using them to fuel the narrative that he was an outsider, someone who had been "canceled" by the mainstream but still loved by his loyal fanbase. He even went so far as to claim that the allegations against him were part of a broader conspiracy to take him down, painting himself as a victim of a corrupt system.

The result was a kind of martyrdom. In the world of SoundCloud rap, where authenticity was prized above all else, XXXTentacion's very public flaws made him seem more real, more relatable, than the polished, PR-friendly rappers who dominated the charts. His legal troubles, his erratic behavior, even his violent temper—they were all part of the same package. He was damaged, and that damage was central to his appeal.

But there's a danger in conflating damage with authenticity, in assuming that because an artist is troubled, their art is somehow more real. Social media has a way of flattening nuance, of turning complex people into caricatures of themselves. And in XXXTentacion's case, the line between his public persona and his private life became so blurred that it was impossible to tell where one ended and the other began.

Was the violence central to his appeal, or was it simply sensationalized by a media eager for clicks? It's hard to say. Certainly, there were fans who defended him even in the face of damning evidence, who claimed that the media was out to get him, that his actions were being blown out of proportion. But there were also those who were drawn to him because of the darkness, because his music—and his life—tapped into something primal and disturbing.

In "Jocelyn Flores," a song that deals explicitly with suicide and depression, XXXTentacion's voice is hauntingly monotone as he describes his own anguish. It's the kind of song that feels deeply personal, almost like a cry for help. And yet, it's hard not to hear the echoes of performativity in it, too. After all, XXXTentacion knew that this kind of vulnerability was what his fans craved. He knew that by sharing his heart, by making it public, he was giving them something they could relate to. But was it real, or was it part of the spectacle?

In many ways, XXXTentacion's career was a case study in the toxic feedback loop of social media fame. The more he shared, the more attention he received; the more attention he received, the more he was compelled to share. It was a cycle that fed on itself, growing larger and more dangerous with each new outburst, each new controversy.

And the media, of course, was complicit in this. Every time XXXTentacion was involved in a fight or arrested for assault, it became headline news. His legal troubles were dissected in gossip columns and social media threads, turning his life into a kind of reality TV show for public consumption.

But for all the attention he garnered, there was always the sense that XXXTentacion, like so many celebrities and ordinary people who get caught up in reality social media exposure, was playing a dangerous game, one that he couldn't win. Fame, especially the kind of fame that is built on controversy, is inherently unstable. It's like building a house on quicksand—eventually, it will collapse under its own weight. And for XXXTentacion, that collapse came all too soon. In June 2018, he was shot and killed in what appeared to be a robbery gone wrong. He was just 20 years old.

In the days and weeks following his death, social media was flooded with tributes from fans and fellow artists alike. But there was also a darker undercurrent to the mourning—a sense of inevitability, as if XXXTentacion's death was simply the logical conclusion to the kind of life in the facst lane that he had been living. He had always been a figure of risk, and in the end, that risk consumed him.

But even in death, XXXTentacion's social media presence continued to haunt the internet. His Instagram account, once a place where he connected directly with his fans, became a shrine of sorts, filled with messages of love and grief. His songs, many of which dealt with themes of death and mortality, took on a new, eerie significance. And his legacy, complicated as it is, became a subject of intense debate.

Was he a victim of his own demons, or a product of a culture that fetishizes violence and trauma? Was he a cautionary tale, or a martyr for a generation that felt just as lost as he did? Or both?

Perhaps the most troubling aspect of XXXTentacion's rise—and his fall—is the way social media not only amplified his flaws but also made them part of his brand. He wasn't just a musician; he was a figure of controversy, a character in the ongoing drama of his own life. And in the world of Instagram and Twitter, where attention is the ultimate currency, that drama was what kept people coming back.

But in the end, the very thing that made XXXTentacion famous—the contradition, the violence, the controversy—was also what destroyed him. His life, and his career, were consumed by the same forces that had fueled his rise. And in the world of social media, where nothing is ever truly forgotten, his legacy remains as complicated as ever.

It's tempting to look at XXXTentacion's story as a cautionary tale, a reminder of the dangers of fame and avatar life in the digital age. But it's also a story about the forces of culture today and the power social media to shape not only how we see artists, but how they see themselves. For XXXTentacion, social media was both a mirror and a magnifying glass, reflecting and amplifying the darkest parts of his life. And in the end, that reflection was too much to bear.

CHAPTER 5

Violence as Style and Story

XXXTentacion's life, both public and private, was entangled with all kinds of violence—a force that shaped his persona, haunted his career, and ultimately contributed to his early death. For fans, media outlets, and critics alike, his music became impossible to separate from the acts of brutality, both physical and symbolic, he both endured and inflicted. The stark contrast between the vulnerability he often displayed in his music and the violence that seemed to trail him in his personal life is one of the most perplexing aspects of XXXTentacion's story, a tension that feels at times irreconcilable.

Born Jahseh Onfroy, XXXTentacion grew up in South Florida under conditions of instability and neglect. The violence that would come to define much of his life began at an early age. He spoke often about his abusive childhood, how his mother, Cleopatra Bernard, left him with relatives, and how he was in constant conflict with other children.

But as much as XXXTentacion's early life was marked by trauma, it was also defined by a capacity for inflicting violence on others. Nowhere is this more evident than in his relationship with Geneva Ayala, his ex-girlfriend and the woman who became the focal point of the most damning chapter of his life. In 2016, Geneva accused XXXTentacion of repeated physical and emotional abuse, including one especially harrowing incident in which he allegedly beat her while she was pregnant. Court documents detailed the brutal assault, describing how XXXTentacion allegedly held her captive, threatened her life, and assaulted her in a way that left her permanently traumatized.

This was no longer the narrative of a troubled artist struggling with internal demons—this was a public revelation of cruelty that placed XXXTentacion in a different category altogether. Geneva Ayala became a symbol of the hidden cost of his fame and the secondary victim his own abuse. She became the young woman who had suffered in silence while XXXTentacion's star was on the rise. In an interview with the *Miami New Times*, Ayala described how her life was forever changed by the abuse, painting a picture of a relationship filled with manipulation, gaslighting, and fear. "He knew how to make me feel like nothing," she said. "He made me feel like I was crazy for thinking he would hurt me."

The reaction to the allegations was polarizing, to say the least. On one side, many in the media—especially mainstream outlets like *Pitchfork* and *The New York Times*—condemned XXXTentacion for his actions, calling him a danger to society and questioning how someone with such a violent history could have a platform at all. For them, the allegations against him weren't just a scandal—they were proof of a deep moral failing. *Pitchfork* was particularly scathing in its coverage of the court proceedings, publishing detailed accounts of Ayala's injuries and the specific charges XXXTentacion faced.

Yet, his fanbase remained largely loyal, with many questioning the validity of the allegations or downplaying their significance. For them, XXXTentacion's pain—the same pain he frequently discussed in his music—justified or at least contextualized his violence. Fans flooded social media with messages of support, pointing to songs like "Revenge" as proof that he was a product of his circumstances, that his violent outbursts were simply the manifestations of a deeply damaged individual trying to navigate a world that had been cruel to him from the start. To these fans, Geneva Ayala became an inconvenient narrative, one that threatened to derail the connection they felt with an artist who spoke to their own struggles with depression, anger, and alienation.

But even beyond his direct relationship with Ayala, XXXTentacion's music was riddled with allusions to violence, both inflicted and endured. Songs like "Revenge," for instance, present an ambiguous relationship with the concept of retribution and suffering. "Revenge on my body, revenge on my heart, revenge on my soul," he sings, with a haunting repetition that seems to invoke both the desire for vengeance and the toll it takes on the self. The title itself suggests a cycle of violence, one that is difficult to escape once entered. There's a numbness to the way he delivers these lines, a kind of resignation to the inevitability of violence in his life, as if it's not just something he does but something that happens to him, a force beyond his control.

In "I Don't Even Speak Spanish LOL," a track that deviates from his typical style with its reggaeton beats and light-hearted feel, the lyrics take on an unexpected significance when viewed in the context of his personal life. While the song may seem like a playful departure, there's an eerie undercurrent to the way he moves between personas—the carefree lover in the song and the violent figure outside of the studio. It's a dissonance that speaks to the complexity of his character and the troubling ways in which he compartmentalized different aspects of his life.

What makes XXXTentacion's violence particularly difficult to process is the extent to which it was woven into the public's perception of him. His legal troubles, his public fights, his outbursts on social media—these were not separate from his music; they were part of the same life/performance. In the digital age, where platforms like Instagram and YouTube allow fans constant access to an artist's personal life, the boundary between Jahseh Onfroy the person and XXXTentacion the performer became blurred to the point of non-existence. This was a new kind of celebrity, one where authenticity was both demanded and manufactured in real-time.

His violence, then, wasn't just a scandal to be reported on—it became central to his mythos, something that both repelled and attracted his audience. This is the paradox at the heart of his career: the more violent and erratic he became, the more people seemed drawn to him. His life became a kind of spectacle, a performance of suffering and brutality that mirrored the chaotic world of social media, where every outburst and every transgression was amplified for maximum effect. We tell ourselves stories in order to live, in order to explain ourselves to ourselves and to others. And we tell ourselves stories to explain the world. Or maybe to explain it away. In the case of XXXTentacion, the story that was told—by him, by the media, and by his fans—was one of a tortured artist whose violence was both a product of his pain and a form of catharsis.

But what does it mean to consume violence as entertainment? For decades, critics have debated the role of violence in art, particularly in music. Artists from Tupac to to Fifty Cent to Eminem have faced backlash for glorifying violence in their lyrics, even as fans defend their work as reflections of the harsh realities of life. In XXXTentacion's case, the debate takes on a new urgency because the violence wasn't just in the music—it was in the man himself. When fans listened to songs like "Revenge," they weren't just hearing a narrative of abstract suffering; they were hearing the voice of someone who had inflicted real pain on others, someone whose actions had left a permanent mark on those around him.

The music industry itself has long been complicit in this dynamic, profiting off the personas of troubled, violent men while turning a blind eye to the damage they cause. In the case of XXXTentacion, record labels, managers, and promoters continued to work with him even after the details of his abuse became public. It's a pattern we've seen before—R. Kelly, Chris Brown, even Michael Jackson—all men whose immense talent was overshadowed by their violent behavior, and yet who continued to enjoy commercial success because the industry deemed them too valuable to lose.

But perhaps what's most troubling about XXXTentacion's legacy is the way in which his violence has been posthumously reframed as part of his artistic narrative. After his death, fans rushed to canonize him, painting him as a martyr for a generation struggling with mental health issues, economic violence, depression, and trauma. His aggressive behavior was downplayed or dismissed as the actions of a young man who didn't know any better, someone who was still trying to find his way in a world that had been unkind to him. It's a narrative that conveniently erases the pain of his victims, particularly Geneva Ayala, whose life was forever altered by her relationship with him.

In the end, the violence that haunted XXXTentacion was both a symptom of his own trauma and a choice he made, over and over again, to inflict that trauma on others. His music, while often beautiful and vulnerable, cannot be separated from the harm he caused. As much as fans may want to believe that they can separate the art from the artist, the reality is far more complicated. XXXTentacion's violence was not just a part of his life—it was central to his identity as an artist, a fact that raises uncomfortable questions about the role of violence in our culture and the ways in which we celebrate and consume it as entertainment.

Joan Didion once wrote, "I have already lost touch with a couple of people I used to be." In the case of XXXTentacion, it's hard to say if he ever truly had the chance to *lose touch* with the person he was. His life, from beginning to end, was marked by violence—both as a victim and as a perpetrator. And while his music may live on, it will forever be haunted by the shadow of the violence that shaped him. XXXTentacion himself indeed embodied the idea of violence as style and story, fashion and narrative, aesthetic and explanation.

CHAPTER 6

Young Fashion

XXXTentacion—he wasn't just a musician; he was a walking contradiction wrapped in fabric and ink, a kaleidoscope of pain and rebellion. In a world where fashion often serves as a flimsy veneer to mask deeper issues, XXXTentacion ripped through that facade with dreadlocks, tattoos, and an aesthetic that was as loud as it was vulnerable. He became a cultural phenomenon not merely by virtue of his music but through the totally distinct way he chose to present himself to the world—a statement on identity, trauma, and the social constructs that govern both.

The young men of his generation—those who wear oversized hoodies and sagging jeans, who boast skin adorned with artful ink—know that style is not just a fashion choice but a manifesto. For XXXTentacion, every tattoo was a verse of his life, and every piece of clothing was a chapter in a story that fluctuated between chaos and vulnerability. He wore his trauma like a badge, an invitation for the world to confront the darkness that lingered in his mind.

And designers have taken up this challenge (the collective Real Fashion Bomb, shown here, has an entire line based on his look .) Yet, here is the irony: in a culture that celebrates the rebellious outsider, XXXTentacion found himself celebrated and vilified in equal measure. In so many ways this is the quintessential mark of an A-list artist. Jean-Michel Basquiat, Andy Warhol, Damien Hirst, and Pablo Picasso found themselves in the same boat.

Fashion is a language all its own—one that speaks volumes about race, class, gender, and the unspoken hierarchies of society. XXXTentacion's dreadlocks, a crown of defiance, his face tats, serve as a reminder of the complexities of cultural appropriation. For many, his look was an embrace of Black culture; for others, it was an unsettling reminder of a society that commodifies pain without reckoning with its historical roots.

His style mirrored the wildness and chaos of a generation grappling with its identity in a world where representations of race and gender can feel like a cruel joke played on those who refuse to conform.

In America, the world of streetwear thrives on the idea of rebellion, creating a marketplace that blends authenticity with commercialism. The paradox of street fashion is that while it may rise from grassroots movements, it often finds its way into the corporate realm, where major brands exploit the very essence of rebellion for profit. Of course, the look becomes defanged i the wrong hands. Dissent is thus always a hit and run affair.

Consider how XXXTentacion's style—marked by his tattoos, oversized drapes, and a nonchalant attitude—was emblematic of a larger shift in youth culture. Brands like Supreme and Off-White emerged as symbols of status, often co-opting street style, whichXXXTentacion embodied.

Yet, unlike polished labels, XXXTentacion's fashion choices were original, raw, unfiltered, and reflective of a life lived on the edge, a life that resonated deeply with a generation craving authenticity in an increasingly manufactured world. In a way, he was the ultimate post-modern fashionisto.

This aesthetic evolution can be traced to the emergence of the "SoundCloud rap" scene, where artists like Lil Uzi Vert, Lil Pump, and XXXTentacion created a new paradigm that blurred the lines between hip-hop and punk rock, with fashion as an integral component. His influence was palpable at music festivals and urban gatherings, where fans donned similar looks—dreadlocks, face tattoos, and oversized tees—creating a subculture that rejected mainstream standards of beauty and dress. It was a powerful statement, one that declared individuality in a society that often demands conformity.

In this context, the garments worn by his fans transcended mere clothing; they became armor, protecting them from the slings and arrows of a society that often felt alien. Wearing XXXTentacion merchandise was not just an act of fandom; it was a statement of identity. The XXX hoodie, emblazoned with bold graphics, became a talisman for those grappling with their own darkness, a uniform for a generation that often felt misunderstood. In this sense, his merchandise was not merely clothing but an emblem of solidarity, a flag raised high in the face of societal indifference.

But the link between fashion and identity is fraught with tension. As XXXTentacion rose to prominence, the line between admiration and exploitation blurred. Major brands, eager to capitalize on his cultural impact, began to incorporate elements of his style into their collections, often without acknowledgment of the artist's troubled history. In a glaring example of this, a well-known streetwear brand released a collection that mirrored XXXTentacion's signature look—giant silhouettes, vibrant colors, and bold graphics—yet failed to mention the man behind the aesthetic. This phenomenon raises uncomfortable questions: when does fashion homage become appropriation? How do we honor the legacy of an artist without stripping away the complexities of their narrative?

The dynamics of race, gender, and cultural representation play a significant role in understanding the complexities of this appropriation. XXXTentacion's life was a testament to the harsh realities faced by many young Black men in America—a life shaped by systemic violence, trauma, and societal expectations. His fashion choices, rooted in this lived experience, became a rallying point for a generation striving to reclaim its narrative. However, as brands commodify this rebellion, they risk diluting the very essence of what made XXXTentacion's style resonate in the first place.

Moreover, XXXTentacion's impact extended beyond his own image; he sparked conversations about the aesthetics of vulnerability and masculinity in fashion. The traditional notions of masculinity—stoic, unemotional, rigid—were challenged by his open discussions about mental health, depression, and trauma. In this way, his style became a canvas for exploring broader themes, inviting conversations about what it means to be a man, especially a man of color, in a society that often encourages emotional suppression. By wearing his brand, fans embraced the idea that vulnerability is not a weakness but rather a powerful form of self-expression.

As we delve deeper into the cultural landscape that XXXTentacion helped shape, we recognize that the aesthetics of rebellion he cultivated are still in play today. Fashion has become an avenue for social commentary, a way to challenge societal norms and expectations. The brands that have embraced this ethos, such as Fear of God and A Bathing Ape, demonstrate the power of fashion as a medium for expressing identity and rebellion. They encourage a dialogue about the complexities of race, class, and gender, pushing against the boundaries of what it means to be stylish in contemporary society.

XXXTentacion's legacy is a multifaceted one—part musical genius, part cultural icon, and part cautionary tale. He embodied the tensions that define American society, reflecting both the dreams and struggles of a generation grappling with its place in the world. His fashion choices invite us to consider the profound impact of aesthetics on identity, and how the garments we wear can serve as a powerful means of communication.

In reflecting on XXXTentacion's vision of fashion and youth, we confront the uncomfortable truths of our society—about race, identity, and the relentless pursuit of authenticity. His life serves as a prism through which we can examine the complexities of contemporary culture, inviting us to grapple with the tensions that define our existence. In the end, the story of XXXTentacion is not just a narrative about a troubled artist; it is a mirror reflecting the struggles, contradictions, and aspirations of a generation in search of its place in the world.

As we navigate the swirling currents of the modern world, we would do well to remember that fashion is not merely about what we wear but about how we choose to present ourselves in a place that often seeks to define us. And often just as an avatar on a small screen that others, many of whom are strangers, may view for just a few seconds. In this sense, XXXTentacion's vision remains as relevant today as ever—a call to embrace our individuality and confront the complexities that shape our identities. He may have been a controversial figure, but in the end, he was also a deeply human one—his legacy reminds us that the journey toward self-discovery is often messy, chaotic, painful and beautifully authentic.

CHAPTER 7

Redemption Songs

XXXTentacion's story is not just that of a troubled artist—it is a reflection of a generation tangled in the complexities of identity, vulnerability, and societal expectations. His music strikes at the heart of a cultural moment where loneliness has morphed into an epidemic, and the hunger for connection feels almost palpable. "I don't want to be alone. I don't want to be left on my own," he sings in "Changes," a sentiment that resonates like a haunting refrain. Yet, to view him merely as another casualty of fame, another tortured soul cast adrift in the void of social media, is to ignore the larger implications of his work and persona. XXXTentacion articulated the frustrations and fears of a generation that often feels unheard, trapped in a commercial landscape where emotional honesty is both celebrated and vilified.

The digital arena serves as a backdrop to his quest for redemption. Each tweet, Instagram post, and song release becomes a fragment of a larger puzzle, a desperate attempt to connect with fans who find themselves equally adrift. In this vortex, a vital question emerges: did audiences genuinely seek to understand him, or were they merely spectators consuming the spectacle of his suffering? This dynamic is not merely personal; it is emblematic of a broader cultural phenomenon wherein vulnerability is commodified and reduced to a trend.

Take the immediate aftermath of the "Changes" music video release. The visual narrative, coupled with the confessional tone of the lyrics, led many to interpret it as a plea for help. Fans and critics alike dissected the video frame by frame, searching for authenticity in every pixel. "He's a genius," some proclaimed, while others countered with accusations of playing the victim. The need to construct a narrative—one that would fit neatly into our preconceptions of artistry—often overshadowed the complexity of his reality.

Consider "Sad!," a track that propelled him to even greater heights while exposing the core of his internal struggles. The chorus—"I just want to be loved"—resonates deeply, embodying a juxtaposition of vulnerability and bravado. This longing for connection becomes a double-edged sword, where love can simultaneously lift and tear apart. Through these lyrics, it is clear that XXXTentacion was not merely a product of his environment; he was a mirror reflecting the chaos of his generation.

Discussions around his openness about mental health often teetered between admiration and skepticism, blurring the lines of authenticity in an age dominated by social media. "The more he exposes, the more we consume," remarked one commentator, pinpointing the paradox of our time—where the act of revealing becomes a performance. In such an environment, the question of whether XXXTentacion was truly seeking redemption or merely leveraging his vulnerability for fame looms large.

The tumultuous relationship with Geneva Ayala punctuates these discussions, revealing the intricacies of gender dynamics and accountability in a culture that idolizes flawed figures. The allegations against him became as integral to his narrative as his music. Supporters waved flags of forgiveness, while critics demanded accountability. This tension reflects a disturbing tendency to overlook transgressions in the name of artistic genius. One friend remarked, "It's like people wanted to see him fail, but they also wanted to love him for it." This paradox complicates our understanding of celebrity, particularly within the realm of masculinity, where vulnerability is often at odds with societal expectations.

Media obsession with his redemption arc encapsulates a cultural fixation on sensationalism, stripping discussions about mental health of their necessary nuance. Headlines questioning the authenticity of his transformation proliferated, begging the inquiry: can an individual's past actions coexist with a genuine desire for change? XXXTentacion's attempts at redemption were scrutinized relentlessly, each move analyzed under a microscope as if everyone was waiting for him to slip again, to reaffirm their worst fears about fame and its accompanying chaos.

In examining his music, the uncomfortable reality emerges: redemption is messy and fraught. The lyrics of "Revenge" reveal a longing for understanding that transcends mere atonement. "I think I found a way to cope," he sings, an assertion that doubles as a personal testament and a universal acknowledgment of the pain that many endure.

The question of whether XXXTentacion achieved redemption cannot be easily answered. His music, a visceral reflection of his struggles, articulates a yearning for connection and understanding that resonates with many. Yet, his legacy is irrevocably intertwined with the violence that marred it. This contradiction—the tension between the desire for forgiveness and the actions that perpetuated his suffering—lies at the crux of ongoing cultural conversations surrounding mental health, celebrity, and accountability.

To disentangle XXXTentacion's legacy is to confront our discomfort with the complexities of the human experience. His music is both a balm and a challenge, inviting listeners to grapple with their narratives while questioning the societal structures that shape them. The crazy journey through fame, violence, and emotional vulnerability reflects our collective struggle, revealing that redemption is not always just an individual pursuit but a communal reckoning—one that demands empathy, understanding, and a willingness to engage with the uncomfortable truths that permeate our lives.

XXXTentacion's existence compels us to grapple with the paradox of vulnerability in an era where it can be both a source of connection and a commodity. As we navigate this cultural landscape, his music stands as a reminder that the search for redemption is intricate—a chaotic, often elusive endeavor intertwined with the complexities of the human condition. Ultimately, it invites us to confront the delicate interplay between despair and hope, challenging us to question what it truly means to seek forgiveness in a world that often prioritizes the spectacle of suffering over genuine understanding.

CHAPTER 8

Gen Z's Anti-Hero

XXXTentacion is a name that still resonates deeply with the youth culture of today, emerging from a backdrop of personal turmoil and societal unrest. He is a figure of immense devotion and deep controversy, an anti-hero for a generation grappling with complex issues of identity, loss of place, and unmet societal expectations. His fans' unwavering loyalty, despite a litany of scandals and accusations of violence, raises critical questions about what it means to be a hero—or, more aptly, an anti-hero—in the current cultural landscape.

The allure of XXXTentacion is in his unapologetic vulnerability. His lyrics lay bare the anguish of a generation struggling with anxiety and fear, navigating a world that often feels hostile and unforgiving. Songs like "Sad!" and "Changes" cut through the noise with raw emotion, connecting with listeners who feel unseen in their pain. The lyrics serve as an anthem for those wrestling with their own demons, highlighting a profound yearning for understanding and connection.

He desperately wanted to live. This sentiment is echoed in interviews where he candidly spoke about his battles with depression, stating, "I just want to be happy, man. I don't want to die."

Yet, the fervent devotion of his fans exists in stark contrast to his public persona, which was riddled with scandals that paint a picture of a deeply flawed individual. The media coverage oscillated between fascination and condemnation, presenting a unresolved narrative that reflects much broader cultural struggles. In a world where social media amplifies both voices and controversies, XXXTentacion became a lightning rod for debates about accountability, redemption, and the complexities of identity. Fans have crafted a mythology around him that emphasizes personal growth, seeing his past mistakes not as indicators of a villain but as part of a messy, human experience.

This narrative speaks volumes about contemporary American society—a landscape where the lines between hero and villain blur, especially when it comes to figures of cultural significance. The affinity for anti-heroes is not just a product of storytelling; it is a reflection of a generation's frustration with sanitized portrayals of success. In a world rife with images of perfection, the rawness of XXXTentacion's life offers a counter-narrative. He embodies the idea that growth is often nonlinear, that one can oscillate between moments of brilliance and darkness.

As fans cling to the notion of redemption, it raises uncomfortable questions about what we are willing to overlook in our heroes. The fervent support for XXXTentacion may stem from a collective recognition of human imperfection—a desire to embrace those who struggle openly with their flaws. This echoes a broader societal trend where audiences are increasingly drawn to complex figures who challenge traditional norms and expectations. In a culture that has long been obsessed with perfection, the appeal of the anti-hero lies in their capacity to humanize the experience of failure and the pursuit of forgiveness.

The implications of this devotion extend beyond personal narratives, touching on issues of race, fame, class oppression, and the commodification of trauma. XXXTentacion, a young Black man, navigated a space fraught with systemic challenges, where his talent was often overshadowed by his controversies. The scrutiny he faced from both fans and the media is indicative of a larger societal pattern that disproportionately affects Black artists. In an industry that often values marketability over authenticity, his life became a testament to the struggle for recognition amidst a cacophony of judgment.

Moreover, the conversations surrounding XXXTentacion invite scrutiny of the very structures that elevate individuals to fame. What does it mean to idolize someone who has perpetuated cycles of violence and pain? The fan devotion speaks to a larger desire for connection in a fragmented world, yet it also raises critical questions about responsibility and accountability. Are we willing to overlook harmful behavior because it resonates with our own experiences, or does that complicity reflect a deeper societal malaise?

The phenomenon of XXXTentacion illuminates the nuances of American culture, where the intersection of race, class, and violence shapes our understanding of identity. In an era marked by social media's omnipresence, the ability to craft one's narrative has never been more accessible. XXXTentacion's artistry, filled with confessional vulnerability, resonates with a generation eager for authenticity but simultaneously wary of the consequences that accompany public exposure. This complexity plays out in real-time, as fans engage with his music while grappling with cancel culture and the moral implications of his legacy.

The cultural significance of XXXTentacion's music extends beyond the individual; it invites broader conversations about the role of art in shaping societal narratives. His songs become a platform for exploring the complexities of grief, loss, and the human experience. In the wake of the Parkland shooting, his tribute "Hope" stands as a poignant reminder of the power of art to connect and heal, even as it emerges from a troubled past. It's a call to confront the pain that permeates our society, an invitation to engage with difficult truths that are often swept under the rug.

Ultimately, the legacy of XXXTentacion forces us to reconsider our notions of heroism and accountability in an age where the personal and the public are linked. The fervent devotion of his fans reveals their deep-seated desire for connection and understanding—a yearning to find solace in the shared experiences of suffering and redemption. His life and music serve as a mirror reflecting the complexities of American society, urging us to confront our own struggles with identity, violence, and the often-painful journey toward healing. And of course, XXXTentacion was not shy about pointing out the hypocrisy of American narratives associated with justice, class mobility, and equality.

In navigating the contentious waters of fame and legacy, XXXTentacion's story resonates with profound implications for a generation seeking to reconcile their own narratives with the realities of the world around them. His enduring popularity is not merely a celebration of his artistry; it is a testament to the complexity of the human experience, an acknowledgment that even in darkness, there exists the possibility of light. In a way, the inability of fans and media to domesticate the story of XXXTentacion, much less his person, is what seems to have driven his fame. And consciously or not, through his lyrics, XXXTentacion continues to challenge us, inviting us to engage with our own vulnerabilities and to face head-on the broader societal issues that shape our lives.

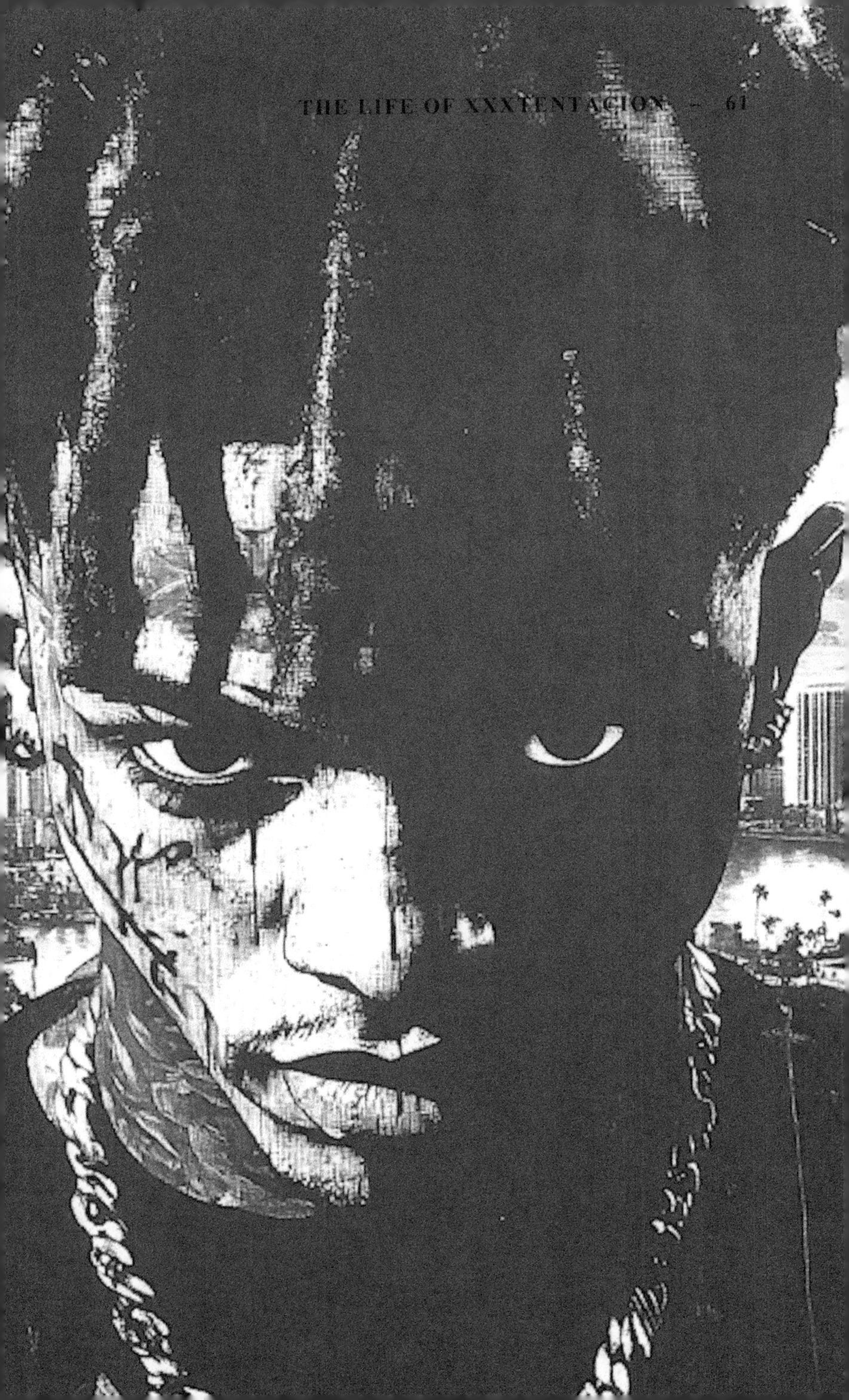

Blaze Carter is a passionate writer and cultural commentator from the streets of South Florida, where the legacy of XXXTentacion continues to resonate. A fan of the artist, Blaze's work explores the relationship between music, identity, and youth culture today. With a keen eye for detail and a knack for storytelling, Blaze explores the emotional landscapes shaped by XXXTentacion's lyrics, addressing themes of vulnerability, rebellion, and redemption. Inspired by the artist's ability to connect with a generation struggling with issues of identity, social justice, and authenticity, Blaze tries to provide insightful analyses that honor XXXTentacion's impact while navigating the controversies surrounding his life. When not writing, he can be found enjoying the underground music scene, engaging in discussions about the evolving nature of fashion and art, and connecting with fellow fans who share a love for the power of music. As a voice for the generation that embraced XXXTentacion's message, Blaze Carter seeks to contribute to the conversation about the artist's lasting influence and the wild cultural landscape we live in.